Monet at Giverny

Patrons of the Fondation Claude Monet-Giverny

Gifts and sponsorship
The restoration of Claude Monet's house and garden has been made possible thanks to the support of many generous patrons, both French and American. Private individuals and organizations wishing to contribute to the upkeep of the house and gardens at Giverny may send gifts to:

Académie des beaux-arts pour la Fondation Claude-Monet
23 quai de Conti
75270 Paris Cedex 06
Tél : 01 44 41 43 20
www.academie-des-beaux-arts.fr

The Versailles Foundation Inc.
Claude Monet Giverny is a nonprofit organization that welcomes tax-exempt contributions and bequests from American taxpayers.
Gifts should be sent to:
The Versailles Foundation Inc. Claude Monet-Giverny
Fondation Claude Monet
420 Lexington Avenue. Suite 1706
New York City, N.Y. 10170
Tél. : (212) 983-3436
vergivinc@gmail.com

Fondation Claude Monet-Giverny
84, rue Claude-Monet
27620 Giverny
www.claude-monet-giverny.fr

Monet at Giverny

Adrien Goetz

Photographs by Éric Sander

éditions Claude Monet Giverny

Preface

When Michel Monet, on his death in 1966, bequeathed his family house at Giverny to the Académie des Beaux-Arts, he was seeking to safeguard memories of his father and to create a place that could be visited by his admirers, who already in the great artist's lifetime were making pilgrimages to Giverny from as far away as Japan and the United States. For the Académie, its acceptance of this gift was a confirmation that it was now also heir to the whole of the anti-Academic tradition of which Claude Monet, the eternal outsider, was the most celebrated embodiment. Thus it was that the bohemians and the outcasts, the maudit rebels and revolutionaries who for so long had stood in opposition to the 'chers maîtres' of the quai de Conti, were admitted to the inner circle presided over by the shades of Poussin, David and Ingres. Michel Monet had chosen not to offer this precious heritage to the Musées de France – perhaps because his father's last works, which with their explosions of pure colour and non-figurative boldness were so far removed from the prettiness of Impressionism, would have been out of place in the Louvre or the Jeu de Paume. The Musée d'Orsay, which was to change the entire landscape, was meanwhile yet to open. But doubtless his motives in the making this bequest were not entirely disingenuous.

The paintings of the Michel Monet bequest were displayed initially in the Musée Marmottan, under the aegis of the Académie; the house at Giverny where Monet had lived from 1883 until his death in 1926 was meanwhile left to stand empty. In the wake of the death of Monet's daughter-in-law Blanche Hoschedé-Monet in 1947 it seemed to have lost its soul, and the gardens had been left to grow wild.

It was not until the arrival of Gérald Van der Kemp, who in 1977 succeeded the architect Jacques Carlu in the unique role of director and curator of Giverny, that patrons began to take an interest in the site, and restoration work could begin. In 1980 the house and garden were opened to the public, and the Fondation Claude-Monet was set up. Armed with the fruits of his experience as the director of Versailles, and with the invaluable support of his wife Florence, herself a corresponding member of the Académie des Beaux-Arts, Gérald Van der Kemp was well versed in the scientific, authentic restoration of historic buildings, and above all in the principles to adopt in the 'restoration' of a historic garden.

Since 2008, I have had the pleasure of continuing the work of Gérald and Florence Van der Kemp, concentrating particularly on the re-creation of the house interiors as they were when the Monet-Hoschedé family lived here. The house and gardens continue to attract visitors in increasing numbers, and for all those who work here the 600,000 visitors who now come to Giverny every year are our greatest reward.

Giverny today remains both popular and fragile. The gardeners, volunteers, administrative, security and reception staff who all work here throughout the year are I believe united in their deep love for the place, the village, and the lyrical beauty of the surrounding countryside. Working with them in order to welcome the public to the Fondation Claude-Monet in the best possible conditions is an exciting challenge. Our gardeners, following in the footsteps of Gilbert Vahé in the time of Gérald Van der Kemp, are all aesthetes and scholars, connoisseurs of both museum collections and botany, and throughout the year we welcome garden-lovers from throughout the world. At the same time, Giverny also functions as a laboratory of both conservation and creation. To walk along its paths and in the shade of its trees is to encounter the shades of Georges Clemenceau and Sacha Guitry, to inhabit a world in which an understanding of nature and a love of art are daily sources of happiness. Yet at the same time this does not imply living in the past: the Académie des Beaux-Arts welcomes artists in residence at Giverny – painters, photographers and writers – who all contribute to the dialogue in which Monet engaged, right to the end of his life, with the young artists of his own time.

This book, the fruit of a close collaboration between a photographer and a writer, reflects this complex and fascinating reality. In this it is much more than a guidebook: rather it is an invitation to view Giverny as more than a glorious setting, a sanctuary or a heritage site frozen in time. These interiors and gardens created by Monet are essentially a work of art: miraculously preserved as living entities, they form an indispensable aid to us in understanding our own modernity.

HUGUES R. GALL,
Member of the Institut (Académie des Beaux-Arts)
Director of the Fondation Claude-Monet

Claude Monet's palette,
preserved in the Musée Marmottan-Monet, Paris.

Walking into a Work of Art

To walk into Monet's house is to enter a small independent realm dedicated to art and nature. This is no memorial where visitors come as pilgrims to worship at a holy shrine; this is a 'creation' in the fullest sense of the word, set at the very heart of an artist's life. Giverny is a microcosm that continues to live to the rhythm of the seasons and flowering times, a world that survives and thrives thanks to the gardeners and volunteers who tend this masterpiece with the all the care of skilled curators and restorers of works of art.

In these interiors, visitors can encounter Monet in his daily life, in his kitchen and dining room, while always remembering that this entertaining host and excellent guest, as warm and welcoming as he was sometimes sombre and troubled, was first and foremost the great artist who with his fellow Impressionists brought about a revolution in late nineteenth-century art. With his *Water Lilies*, painted at Giverny, he opened up new vistas on the verge of abstraction, for twentieth-century art, that were in the first instance – notably through they *Haystack* paintings – to inspire Kandinsky, and later Jackson Pollock, Mark Rothko, Joan Mitchell and Sam Francis.

A visit to Giverny reveals the successive stages in Monet's life, peeling back the chronological layers and enabling us to trace the evolution of a great artist in the very spots where he found his inspiration. It is this overlap between the individual anecdotal detail and the overarching sweep of art history that makes a visit to Giverny such an engrossing experience.

Monet at Giverny was not just the nature lover who created a perfect haven and ideal setting for family life, but also the artist who for so many years was cast out by the establishment before finally gaining recognition, and who hung his walls with significant canvases to create a narrative of his life. The Monet we meet at Giverny is the great artist who hung the upstairs rooms in which he spent his time with the paintings that he loved and wanted to see on a daily basis: works by artists he admired, such as Delacroix; by his fellow artists in the great adventure of Impressionism, from Renoir to Cézanne; and by artists whom he encouraged, such as Signac. Downstairs, meanwhile, he hung the walls of the rooms most used by the family with the Japanese prints of which he was such a passionate collector, which conjure up a world of exotic images of distant lands, and an invitation to penetrate further, into the second garden that lies across the road, around the lily pond that glints like a mirror in the distance.

Rose arches span the central path and frame the house and the wooden steps leading up to it. After recent restoration work, the building now has the appearance once more of an inviting family home. Monet was to transform it into a work of art.

The two gardens thus tell the story of the evolution of Monet's artistic vision and of his work. The first of the two to be planted, the Clos Normand in front of the house, was to provide numerous subjects for his paintings – which in turn have provided references for its meticulous reconstruction. The Japanese-inspired water garden was in its turn to inspire Monet's final paintings, created in the last studio to be built at Giverny, a modern design with a metallic structure and top-lighting. Today the monumental *Water Lilies* paintings are displayed – following Monet's wishes – at the Musée de l'Orangerie in the Tuileries, where they are also bathed in natural light. Rather than being faced with framed paintings hanging on a wall, visitors to the Orangerie find themselves inside a work of art, an 'installation' before its time, surrounded by colour and light – just as they are in the water garden at Giverny, which invites them to meditate on the beauties of nature. Monet rejected the notion of any comparisons between his *Water Lilies* and the circular panoramas that were so popular in the nineteenth century, suggesting the illusion of being at Giverny while in fact standing in central Paris. Rather he had created a work of art that was utterly new and without precedent.

10

The gardens at Giverny stand outside time and space, contrasting with the surrounding natural landscape to form a pioneering and thus all the more essential example of 'land art', to be visited for its own sake, and not simply as an example of the vogue for the Japanese influence in the history of European gardens. We have to be open to the effects of this man-made space that has been constructed with such skill, to lose ourselves among its reflections and shadows, to allow ourselves to be drawn into a microcosm that was first created in order to be painted, and that now stands alone. Giverny lies at the heart of the second major revolution in art history brought about by Monet. This was his final work, a twentieth-century work that reached beyond painting, fifty years after the shock of that first legendary exhibition in 1874 that created Impressionism.

The Japanese bridge, added in 1893 and subsequently draped with wisterias, forms the main axis of the second garden: the water garden. Monet made it the most celebrated feature of the gardens at Giverny by featuring it as an essential element in his compositions, from his first paintings of the lily pond and the bridge in 1899 to his final canvases, after 1918, in which the image of the bridge dissolved in a wild and almost abstract blaze of colours.

A House in the Country for Painting en Plein Air

This country farmhouse, long and plain, delighted Monet. He first came across it on one of the country walks that he enjoyed – as a reader of Jean-Jacques Rousseau – in order to savour the beauties of the countryside and to find subjects for his paintings. The year 1883, when he moved to Giverny, was coincidentally to prove the halfway point of his long life. For Monet it was love at first sight: for the site, the setting and the village, even more than for the house itself, which was architecturally slightly dull when he first saw it. The building was a former *pressoir* that had been turned into a rural dwelling and extended by a barn – later Monet's first studio. The inside of the house had already been decorated in the comfortable eighteenth-century style then in vogue, while the grazing land surrounding it, covering just under a hectare, had been walled around. The house façade had been covered with pink rough-cast, and a central pediment with an oeil-de-boeuf window had been added to give it the more imposing air of a *maison de maître*. The street façade was not much to look at – as befitted any respectable establishment – but the garden façade was more appealing, despite the damp shade cast by the tall trees that Monet was gradually to clear.

In another more symbolic coincidence, 1883 also saw the death of Edouard Manet, the artist whom Monet held in infinite esteem and patron of the Impressionist group – even though had never taken part in their exhibitions. The move to Giverny, which took place partly by boat, was lengthy and complicated and gave Monet endless cause for complaint. Did he realize that the time had now come, after years of wandering and unhappiness, to put a stop to it all, to turn his back on the exhaustions of Paris; that it was time to set himself apart from the world, the better to fill the place of the 'greatest living modern artist', left vacant by Manet's death?

A few years before he died, Monet – who loved to tell the story of his house and to build his own legend in his lifetime – told the writer Marc Elder how it all started: 'I bought the house, and little by little I enlarged it. My drawing room was originally the barn ... In the garden we all set to: I would dig, plant and hoe, and in the evening the children would water. As things improved, so I expanded. One day I managed to cross the road and start work on this garden [the water garden and lily pond].' He was at pains to point out that Giverny was above all his own creation, made with the labour of his own hands.

The tulips in the foreground were among Monet's favourite flowers, and he travelled to Holland to paint them growing en masse in the tulip fields. The ground-floor rooms of the house opened on to the wooden verandah, allowing the family to extend their living space into this sunny terrace between the house and garden. Monet had written of his yearning for a 'permanent home'; now he had found his haven at last.

Monet's biographer Marianne Alphant has stressed the contrast that existed between the sixty-year-old Monet, who by 1900 had found at Giverny a safe haven where he could live the life of a gentleman farmer, and the tortured artist, plagued by doubts, darkness and rage, that he still remained underneath. The letters he wrote giving orders to his gardener at Giverny demonstrate clearly that he was master of himself and his world, confident of what he wanted and unchallenged in his judgments. In front of his paintings, by contrast, he suffered agonies of indecision and doubt, and was sometimes reduced to scratching and tearing at the canvas, racked by spasms of rage that were both destructive and creative. It is a paradox that sums up Monet's character: the patriarch of Giverny, surrounded by happy children, contented servants and wise gardeners, had deliberately created a house and garden that were not in his image. When he wanted to paint, moreover, he would take himself off elsewhere – to Bordighera in Italy, for instance, of which he wrote, 'You've never seen me at work when I'm on my own and far away like this.' From 1900, as old age

encroached on him, he spent all his time at Giverny; but he was still prey to his dark moods, and now he would shut himself away in his upstairs rooms for days at a time, while the house lay under a blanket of silence, and everyone tiptoed around him. His stepson Jean-Pierre Hoschedé described how awkward it could be: 'At table no one would move or speak, and the only sound was the scraping of forks on plates. Then when he reappeared, usually at my mother's entreaty, the atmosphere would gradually lift and everything went back to normal. Then Monet would spend all his time outside in his gardens.'

The central pediment pierced with a bull's eye adds an elegant touch, transforming a solid farmhouse into an attractive country house in the eighteenth-century style – a taste that was very much in vogue in a France that was becoming increasingly modern and industrialized from the 1860s.

The Blue Salon and the Japanese Print Collection

Monet painted the ground-floor rooms in the blue and yellow colour scheme that he so loved, highlighting and outlining their architectural features and drawing the light into the building, and transforming the farmhouse into something resembling a small manor house, complete with simple woodwork, grandfather clock and traditional furniture. At a period when decorations tended to be dark, with a great deal of natural wood and wallpapers in fussy patterns or faux Cordoba leather, from the moment the visitor set foot in the hall the message of this strikingly original decorative scheme was unmistakable: this was the house of the master of light in painting.

The first feature that strikes the visitor is the collection of Japanese prints of which Monet was particularly proud and that lent a visual unity to the sequence of ground-floor rooms. This was more than a country house: it was a manifesto. The famous Ukiyo-e – 'images of the floating world' – create a world within a world, plunging us into a different realm of images, an inspiration for the paintings of Monet and his Impressionist friends, and taking us back to the final years of his life, when he painted the *Water Lilies*.

As he showed Marc Elder his print collection Monet explained: 'And what you see here is only a part of it. I still have so many boxes of them! ... I wish I could put more of them

Utamaro (c. 1753-1806), *Owl and Two Eastern Bullfinches* **(1791),**
Fondation Claude Monet-Giverny

on display. I should have had portfolio frames made for them, so that I could change the prints whenever I wanted to [...] I have many admirers in Japan, you know. They often come here, and sometimes they pay me the delightful compliment of bringing their wives with them, dressed in traditional Japanese costume. How magnificent their robes are! On one occasion, a car carrying with these precious creatures rolled off the road near Bonnières. We had to go and gather up the ladies. Well, those Japanese visitors weren't the least surprised to find my house lined with their prints. And when I said to them, in front of one of my paintings, "It won't mean much to you, I suppose?" they replied: "More than you might imagine. Your art is not so far removed from that of our masters."' The similarities between Hokusai's *Sazai Pavilion of the Temple of the Five Hundred Rakan*, owned by Monet, and his own *Garden at Sainte-Adresse* are well documented..

A far cry from the 'Trianon grey' that was then so fashionable in Paris interiors, these elegant shades of blue complement Monet's collection of Japanese prints. The grandfather clock and buffet used as a bookcase have been painted to match the woodwork, so that they discreetly blend into the background. The sofa offers an invitation to read and daydream beneath these distant images of a floating world.

For obvious reasons of conservation, these fragile works on paper have been replaced by facsimiles. These give a clear idea of the scale of the collection, which contained 231 prints and rivalled those of the other great pioneers in this field, Bracquemond, Manet, Rodin and Van Gogh. Monet was one of a group of collectors that also included the writers and critics Gustave Geffroy and Théodore Duret. He possessed a number of great masterpieces, often in editions of excellent quality, including Utamaro's *Young Woman applying Make Up*, which he hung in the dining room; Hokusai's *Under the Wave, off Kanagawa*; and Hiroshige's *Sudden Shower over Shin-ohashi Bridge and Atake* in the hall. Monet was able pick out artists of major importance, and favoured subjects that spoke to him: there were few portraits of theatrical faces, for instance, but rather landscapes such as Hokusai's magnificent *Snow on the Sumida River* in the dining room; flower studies, naturally, including chrysanthemums, peonies and morning glories; traditional costumes; and entertaining scenes showing western figures.

Monet related how he had first come across Japanese prints on a trip to Holland in 1871, when he had seen a dealer in the city of Zaandam using Utamaro and Hokusai prints as wrapping paper. He also claimed to have bought Japanese prints at the port of Le Havre as early as 1856, when he was just sixteen. Throughout his life he was an extremely skilled collector, collecting complete sets of prints and making shrewd purchases of works that were already becoming sought after. In 1892, Edmond de Goncourt reported that he had bumped into Monet 'in the little attic of Japanese prints' at the art dealer Samuel Bing's premises, and the Japanese art dealer Tadamasa Hayashi, who had settled in Paris after the Exposition Universelle in 1867, was a frequent visitor at Giverny.

Utamaro (c.1753-1806),
Young Woman applying Make Up (c.1795-6),
Fondation Claude Monet-Giverny

Hokusai (1760-1849), *Snow on the Sumida River*, from the series *Snow, Moon and Flowers (Setsugekka)*, Fondation Claude Monet-Giverny

When choosing Japanese prints, Monet favoured landscapes. The outstanding collection he created not only bears the stamp of true connoisseur, but also forms a link between the house and the Japanese inspiration of the water garden.

Hiroshige (1797-1858), *Sudden Shower over Shin-ohashi Bridge and Atake*,
Fondation Claude Monet-Giverny

The Drawing Room Studio, Monet's First Studio

This was the first of Monet's three successive studios at Giverny. From 1899 he converted the studio into a salon, which the works he hung on the walls turned into something of a shrine dedicated to his paintings. As he explained to Marc Elder, 'These are old memories in this room. They matter to me; I like to have them around me. As far as possible – and it hasn't always been easy! – I have kept a painting from every stage of my life. As you see, there are paintings of the beaches of Normandy, England, Norway, Bell-Ile, the Seine – that one's the ice-melt in front of my house – the south of France, Italy, my garden ...'

Hugues Gall, director of the Fondation Claude-Monet, has continued inside the house the work that Gérald and Florence Van der Kemp undertook in the gardens, re-creating the original interiors and enabling us to picture how the rooms looked in Monet's time. Visitors are warned that the paintings they see here are reproductions (created by the Galerie Troubetzkoy in Paris) of originals that now hang in the Musée Marmottan-Monet, the Musée d'Orsay and other great museums and galleries throughout the world. They are seeing them just as Monet arranged them, however: the authenticity of the hanging scheme lies in its overall effect and its re-creation of Monet's own plans. It emerges clearly that his intentions were far more than merely decorative: this hanging scheme is in fact a primary source for Monet's own vision of his life and career and the way he presented them to his visitors. Thanks to Sylvie Patin, general curator at the Musée d'Orsay and corresponding member of the Académie des Beaux-Arts, with the aid of interior designer Hubert Le Gall, sixty facsimiles of paintings by Monet have been hung as in photographs taken in 1915 and 1920. In this room, Monet displayed the major periods in his artistic career, while at the same time adding recent paintings on an easel, so that he could show them to friends and his dealers. The layout of the room is as Alice and Claude Monet would have known it, with an upholstered couch, cane chairs, a writing desk, and wooden packing cases designed to hold the paintings when they were sent to exhibitions. On closer examination, this is in fact a very bold hanging scheme. This is no bourgeois salon: many of the paintings are unframed, and this is clearly an artist's collection. Many of the works date from the difficult years when Monet was battling for recognition and struggling for survival. His first wife Camille appears in *The Red Cape*, painted in 1873 (Cleveland Museum of Art) and almost certainly on the beach at Trouville (Musée Marmottan-Monet). And above all, they include Monet's painting of her on her deathbed in 1879 (Musée d'Orsay). This painting hangs opposite the sofa, where it is easy to imagine Monet's second wife Alice – who had nursed Camille devotedly until her death – sitting with a cup of tea. Monet kept paintings that were significant to him, works that enable us to understand how, after the Impressionist period, he conceived of his cycles of paintings, with examples here including some of the *Haystacks* series and one of the *Cathedral* series. Also here are successful paintings done on his travels, to Cap Martin in

1884, to London in the 1900s (here represented by several works), to Norway in 1895, and to Venice with Alice in 1908. He thus created a sort of ideal map of his life. Between these paintings he slotted in, in no apparent order, paintings that reflected Giverny back to itself, concentric voyages in miniature around his house and garden, painted on this spot and brought together in this holy of holies: one of the circular *Water Lilies* paintings, and others of the water garden and other views. And according to the young Suzanne Hoschedé, pictures of little Jean on his horse and two paintings of *Woman with a Parasol* were at once both family portraits and masterpieces of art.

Claude Monet in his drawing room studio in 1915.

Framing the garden with its ever-changing colours, the window seems to open up a living painting in the wall. Initially Monet's studio, this room became the room in which he liked to entertain visiting friends with tales from his life, in the form of commentaries on the paintings he had hung on the walls. Here he created a private exhibition of the paintings that meant the most to him.

'These are old memories'

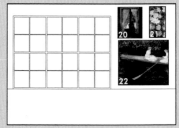

1. *Fishing Boats, Etretat*, 1885, Honfleur, Musée Eugène-Boudin, Gift of Michel Monet, 1964
2. *View of Rouen*, 1892, Rouen, Musée des Beaux-Arts
3. *Cap Martin*, 1884, Private Collection
4. *The Artist's Garden at Vétheuil*, 1881, Washington, National Gallery of Art
5. *Rouen Cathedral, Façade (Sunset)*, 1892, Paris, Musée Marmottan Monet, Michel Monet Bequest, 1966
6. *Water Lilies, Evening Effect*, 1897-9, Paris, Musée Marmottan Monet, Michel Monet Bequest, 1966
7. *île de la Grande Jatte*, 1878, Tokyo, Nichido Gallery
8. *Field of Yellow Irises at Giverny*, 1887, Paris, Musée Marmottan Monet, Michel Monet Bequest, 1966
9. *Boats in the Port of Honfleur (sketch)*, 1917, Paris, Musée Marmottan Monet, Michel Monet Bequest, 1966
10. *Norwegian Landscape, Blue Houses*, 1895, Paris, Musée Marmottan Monet, Michel Monet Bequest, 1966
11. *Charing Cross Bridge*, 1899-1901, Indianapolis Museum of Art
12. *Charing Cross Bridge (sketch)*, 1899-1901, Paris, Musée Marmottan Monet, Michel Monet Bequest, 1966
13. *Poly, Fisherman at Belle-île*, 1886, Paris, Musée Marmottan Monet, Michel Monet Bequest,1966
14. *The Creuse Valley, Evening Effect*, 1889, Paris, Musée Marmottan Monet, Michel Monet Bequest, 1966
15. *Charing Cross Bridge, Smoke in the Fog, Impression*, 1899-1901, dated 1902, Paris, Musée Marmottan Monet, Michel Monet Bequest, 1966
16. *Houses of Parliament, Reflctions in the Thames*, 1900-1, dated 1905, Paris, Musée Marmottan Monet, Michel Monet Bequest, 1966
17. *Pink Water Lilies*, 1897-9, Rome, Galleria Nazionale d'Arte Moderna
18. *Haystack*, 1891, France, Private Collection
19. *Three Fishing Boats*, 1885, Private Collection
20. *The Red Cape (Madame Monet)*, 1873, Cleveland Museum of Art
21. *White Clematis*, 1887, Paris, Musée Marmottan Monet, Michel Monet Bequest, 1966
22. *Boating on the River Epte*, 1890, São Paulo, Museu de Arte Assis Chateaubriand
23. *Three Trees in Summer*, 1891, Tokyo, National Museum of Western Art
24. *Bouquet of Mallows*, 1880, exposé aux Courtauld Institute Galleries, Londres
25. *Corner of the Pond at Giverny*, 1917, Musée de Grenoble, Gift of Claude Monet, 1923
26. *The Castle of Dolceacqua*, 1884, Paris, Musée Marmottan Monet, Michel Monet Bequest, 1966
27. *Bazille and Camille (study for Le Déjeuner sur l'herbe)*, 1865, Washington, National Gallery of Art
28. *Water Lilies*, 1903, Paris, Musée Marmottan Monet, Michel Monet Bequest, 1966
29. *A Field of Tulips in Holland*, 1886, Paris, Musée Marmottan Monet, Michel Monet Bequest, 1966
30. *Study of a Figure Outdoors : Woman with a Parasol, facing right*, 1886, Paris, Musée d'Orsay, Gift of Michel Monet to the Musée du Louvre, 1927
31. *Study of a Figure Outdoors : Woman with a Parasol, facing left*, 1886, Paris, Musée d'Orsay, Gift of Michel Monet to the Musée du Louvre, 1927
32. *The Pink Rowing Boat*, 1890, Private Collection
33. *Vase of Flowers*, 1882, Philadelphia Museum of Art

51

18

8

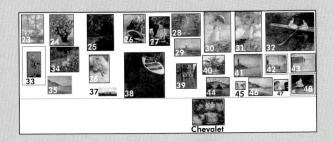 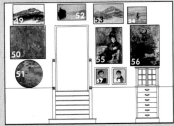

Chevalet

34. *The Garden at Giverny*, 1895, Zurich, Bührle Collection and Foundation
35. *Beach at Pourville, Sunset*, 1882, Paris, Musée Marmottan Monet, Michel Monet Bequest, 1966
36. *Camille on her Deathbed*, 1879, Paris, Musée d'Orsay, Gift of Katia Granoff to the Musée du Jeu de Paume, 1963
37. *Haystacks at Chailly at Sunrise*, 1865, San Diego Museum of Art
38. *The Boat*, 1887, Paris, Musée Marmottan Monet, Michel Monet Bequest, 1966
39. *Palazzo Dario, Venice*, 1908, Private Collection
40. *Palm Tree at Bordighera*, 1884, Private Collection
41. *Sunset in Venice*, 1908, Tokyo, Bridgestone Museum of Art, Ishibashi Foundation
42. *Red Boats, Argenteuil*, 1870, Paris, Musée de l'Orangerie, Walter-Guillaume Collection, 1963
43. *Cliffs of the Porte d'Aval*, 1884, Basle, Kunstmuseum
44. *The Seine at Port-Villez*, 1885, Cologne, Wallraf-Richartz-Museum
45. *On the Beach at Trouville*, 1870, Paris, Musée Marmottan Monet, Michel Monet Bequest, 1966
46. *Cliffs at PourvilleSunset*, 1896, Vernon, Musée Municipal A.-G. Poulain, Gift of Michel Monet, 1964
47. *The Beach at Trouville*, 1870, London, National Gallery
48. *Jean Monet on his Hobby Horse*, 1872, Japan, Sara Lee Corporation

On the easel
  The Japanese Bridge, 1918-1919, Paris, Musée Marmottan Monet, Michel Monet Bequest, 1966
49. *Mount Kolsaas, Norway*, 1895, Paris, Musée Marmottan Monet, Michel Monet Bequest, 1966
50. *Weeping Willow*, 1918-1919, Paris, Musée Marmottan Monet, Michel Monet Bequest, 1966
51. *Water Lilies*, 1908, tondo, Vernon, Musée Municipal A.-G. Poulain, Gift of Claude Monet to the town of Vernon, 1925
52. *The Seine at Port-Villez, Evening Effect*, 1894, Paris, Musée Marmottan Monet, Michel Monet Bequest, 1966
53. *Mount Kolsaas, Norway*, 1895, Paris, Musée d'Orsay
54. *The Sailing Boat, Evening Effect*, 1885, Paris, Musée Marmottan Monet, Michel Monet Bequest, 1966
55. *Camille holding a Posy of Violets*, 1876-7, Private Collection
56. *Camille et Jean Monet in the Garden at Argenteuil*, 1873, Private Collection
57. *Jean Monet*, 1880, Paris, Musée Marmottan Monet, Michel Monet Bequest, 1966
58. *Michel Monet in a Blue Jumper*, 1883, Paris, Musée Marmottan Monet, Michel Monet Bequest, 1966

34
38
46

An Extended Family

At Giverny, Alice and Claude Monet – who were not married until 1892 – raised a family that was happy, complicated and highly unconventional for its time, which today we would describe as an extended family. Monet had spent the most impecunious years of his life with the beautiful and romantic Camille Doncieux (1847-1879), of whom little is known except that she married him in 1870 and bore him two sons, Jean (1867-1914) and Michel (1878-1966). Michel married Gabrielle Bonaventure in 1927 and had no children, and it was he who bequeathed Giverny to the Académie des Beaux-Arts.

Monet's second great love was Alice Raingo (1844-1911), who came from a wealthier background and in 1863 had married Ernest Hoschedé (1838-1891), a great art lover and enlightened collector, who had the courage to buy, among other major paintings, *Impression: Sunrise*, the painting that when presented to the public in 1874 lent its name to Impressionism (Musée Marmottin-Monet). Hoschedé's ruin, which plunged him into despair and meant that he was no longer able to support his family,

and Monet's loss of Camille, which left him devastated and destitute, brought Alice and Claude together. After an unusual period of communal living, during which Ernest Hoschedé continued to play a paternal role, Monet the penniless painter became almost despite himself a figure of central importance for both sets of siblings. The two families lived together for a while at Vétheuil and in a wretched little house at Poissy, before Monet found sanctuary at Giverny, so perpetuating an ambivalent arrangement that was very much on the fringes of the social and moral conventions of the period. Alice nursed Camille, and Hoschedé admired Monet; Monet respected Hoschedé in turn, and Alice was more of an intellectual who knew her own mind than a woman of easy virtue. Pious and traditional in her views, she moved from one man to the other with the utmost consideration and without compromising the strict decorum with which she conducted herself.

Alice and Ernest Hoschedé had four daughters and two sons. In 1897, their second child, Blanche (1865-1941), married Claude and

——— marries in 1892 ———

Camille née **Doncieux** marries in 1870 **Claude Monet**
(1847-1879)   (1840-1926)

Children of **Camille** and **Claude**

Jean   **Michel**
(1867-1914)   (1878-1966)
                             marries in 1927

Gabrielle Bonaventure
(1890-1964)

——— marries in 1897 ———

Camille's son Jean. Monet considered his daughter-in-law as his daughter, and inspired her to go with him on his painting expeditions in the countryside. Her bedroom, on the first floor, bears witness to her tastes and to her attachment to this house, where she was the last of the family to live.

Blanche Hoschedé-Monet's brothers and sisters – Marthe (1864-1925), Suzanne (1868-1899), Jacques (1869-1941), Germaine (1873-1968) and Jean-Pierre (1877-1961) – all lived with Monet after he became their mother's partner. When in 1892 Suzanne Hoschedé, the model for *Woman with a Parasol*, decided to marry Theodore Butler (1861-1936), an American artist who was working at Giverny, Claude Monet married Alice, who had been a widow for a year, in a discreet ceremony. A year after Suzanne's death, Theodore married her elder sister Marthe. Suzanne and Theodore Butler's children included the fashion designer Lily Butler, who was in turn the mother of the painter Jean-Marie Toulgouat, born at Giverny (1927-2006). With his wife

Claire Joyes, Jean-Marie Toulgouat contributed to the restoration of the house and gardens through the many documents in his possession, when Gérald Van der Kemp launched his major appeals for funds from French sponsors.

Germaine Monet married Albert Salerou (1873-1954) in 1902, and was the grandmother of the historian and art critic Philippe Piguet (born 1946), who looks back on his remarkable family as a 'microcosm', created with as much affection and determination as that other microcosm, Giverny itself. This was a world apart, created by Monet and protected against incursions from the outside world; a world in which a 'perfect' family of eight children lived in the midst of a perfect garden, under the benign dictatorship of a master who imposed his own timetable and moods, as well as his fatherly love, which made up for everything. He always signed off his letters to Alice's six children, *'Je t'embrasse comme je t'aime, ton vieux père Claude Monet'* ('I kiss you as I love you, your old father Claude Monet').

Alice *née* **Raingo** marries in 1863 **Ernest Hoschedé**
(1844-1911)   (1838-1891)

Children of **Ernest** and **Alice**

Marthe	**Blanche**	**Suzanne**	**Jacques**	**Germaine**	**Jean-Pierre**
(1864-1925)	(1865-1947)	(1868-1899)	(1869-1941)	(1873-1968)	(1877-1961)
marries in 1900		marries in 1892	marries in 1896	marries in 1902	marries in 1903
Theodore Earl Butler		**Theodore Earl Butler**	**Inga Jürgensen**	**Albert Salerou**	**Geneviève Costaldeau**
(1861-1936)		(1861-1936)	(1862-1944)	(1873-1954)	(1874-1957)

James   Lily
(1893-1976)   (1894-1949)

Simone   Nitia
(1903-1986)   (1909-1964)

The Epicerie: the World in Spices

This little room occupies a place of central importance in the house. The prints on the walls are images of trade between the Orient and the West, and the armoire contains a range of spices in a palette of colours that recalls an artist's paintbox, whisking the visitor off on an armchair tour of exotic lands. This is where the cook and housemaid would come to fetch delicacies such as teas from London, Bourbon vanilla pods from the island of Réunion, cinnamon from Ceylon (Sri Lanka) and cloves. The aromatic scents of the spices and condiments stored here mingled with the floral fragrances of the garden to create a heady paradise of all the senses for guests at Giverny.

The functional rooms in the house are also harmonious and aesthetic in their design. The prints on the walls of the spice store or larder illustrate the trading links between the West and the Far East.

When he visited Monet at Giverny, the art dealer René Gimpel was struck by the kitchen, with its 'lovely blue tiles, so spotless and delectable'.

The Kitchen: Modern Conveniences and Rouen Tiles

The most striking feature of the kitchen is its blue-and-white ceramic tiles from Rouen, with woodwork painted in blue gloss. This room is a favourite with contemporary visitors, who admire its battery of gleaming copper pans, including preserving pans, frying pans, sauté pans, casserole dishes, bains-marie, fish kettles and serving platters. There was no place for exoticism or Japanese style in the kitchen: Monet's guests would have taken no interest in his kitchen arrangements, and Monet himself – taking the mores of 'respectable' houses as his model – would have kept a suitable distance when supervising the preparation of the succulent chickens and andouillettes he so enjoyed. He put complete trust in his cooks, Caroline, Mélanie and the legendary Marguerite, who stayed on after Monet's death to cook for Blanche. A window opening on to the street enabled the kitchen staff to supervise deliveries, while steps to one side led down to the cellar – which did not run under the whole building – where they could give their full attention to the selection of wines. Two windows and a pair of french windows opened on to the garden, allowing fresh air to circulate freely in this practical and modern kitchen.

The Dining Room, 'bathed in golden sunshine'

Monet loved the pleasures of the table. His favourite dishes included asparagus, roast duck, well-hung woodcock and partridge, and salads liberally anointed with oil and seasoned with pepper. Visitors such as Marc Elder painted a rosy (possibly too rosy?) picture of harmonious family life in this room, 'bathed in golden sunshine that filters through the rose arches outside the windows', in an image reminiscent of an Impressionist painting: 'The slightly blowsy cheerfulness of the garden became more muted in the cool intimacy of the interior of the house. The table was more than welcoming, more than a family affair. In the company of the master one felt light and easy of heart, nurtured by affection and peace of mind. "Are you fond of rhubarb? Dash it, here's the secret of this magnificent gateau..."' The American artist Lilla Cabot Perry described how Monet liked to open the windows to feed the birds, on one occasion pointing out to her one of his 'lodgers' with a damaged claw, a faithful visitor for three years.

This spacious room was designed to accommodate no more than a dozen or so guests. This was not a space for grand receptions or formal parties, but rather a private room for the family, into which visiting friends – always aware of the honour that was being granted to them – would sometimes be invited. This was where the whole family sat down to lunch at 12.30 on the dot, the time ordained by Monet even if it meant that the children had to come home from school early. The floor of red-and-white St Just tiles is a typically rustic feature, simple and serviceable. A single touch of profound originality is added by the chrome yellow paint on every surface, which somehow transforms the room into a painterly space. Here the distinction between a 'major artist' and a 'decorative artist' is blurred: for Monet, who persisted in calling his brilliant *Water Lily* paintings 'my large decorative pieces', there was nothing beneath him about transforming the interiors of his house with his chosen palette of colours – quite the contrary, in fact.

The two tall silver cabinets from the Pays de Caux each contain a dinner service – one for everyday use and the other a more valuable Creil service in a Japanese-inspired design – and a few rare pieces, including ceramic wares from Rouen and Delft, as well as others imported from the Far East by the French East India Company. On the sideboards stand a valuable Swiss clock, a tobacco pot, green Vallauris vases and a delicately modelled Japanese figure of a snoozing cat.

Two sets of French windows hung with white broderie anglaise curtains gave access to the garden in summer. Two flower-holders, one from Rouen and the other Japanese, stand between the windows, beside a Ming vase. A green-painted wooden balustrade stretches the length of the building, making an ideal spot for enjoying coffee or a drink in the sun, or for taking family photographs. It also acts as a viewpoint over the garden, and a bridge forming part of the dialogue between inside and outside. The painting *Garden at Sainte-Adresse*, painted before Impressionism, in 1867, displays a similar structure, with a foreground stretching parallel to the horizon – though here the garden replaces the sea.

The intense colour scheme chosen by Monet for the dining room and detailed in a painter's bill of 1914 – 'light chrome yellow, with mouldings picked out in pure chrome yellow' – remains in place today. The two dinner services used alternately in Monet's time are also still here.

Distinguished Friends and Guests

While he was a warm and welcoming host, Monet could also be discouraging to visitors. Philippe Piguet recorded the memories of his mother Simone Salerou (1903-1986), who spent the school year of 1914-15 at Giverny: 'Sometimes, when his painting would not come as he wanted it to, he would get very angry, and I saw him fly into terrible rages.' The classic bourgeois plea to boisterous children to 'go and play in the garden' did not apply here: Monet discouraged the younger members of the family from taking their friends into the garden, and even forbade them from addressing the flowers with the familiar 'tu', as little Claude Renoir, son of Auguste, once dared to do.

The villagers did not enjoy a good relationship with the Monet clan and did not welcome them among them, while Monet did nothing to encourage them to visit. The sole exception was Abbé Toussaint, who became a friend both of the staunchly Catholic Alice and of the equally staunchly anti-clerical Monet – a conviction the artist shared with his friend Georges Clemenceau.

An inner circle of friends who were always welcome included Auguste Renoir, Octave Mirbeau (the author of *Diary of a Chambermaid*, who braved the cold to come to Giverny on 1 January 1909 to view the canvases Monet had brought back from Venice) and of course Clemenceau. Monet made no concessions to their presence, veering between abject despondency, fits of rage and friendly enthusiasm. Stéphane Mallarmé, Paul Valéry, Thadée and Misia Natanson and Sacha Guitry might all be found at Giverny: Monet liked writers, particularly members of the Académie Goncourt, of which he was sometimes the guest of honour. He was close to the novelist Lucien Descaves, now largely forgotten, and possessed a number of his works with handwritten dedications. Dealers such as Paul Durand-Ruel, and Josse and Gaston Bernheim also came, as did the great American painters Whistler and Sargent. And Monet had his photograph taken at Giverny with his Japanese friends Mr and Mrs Kuroki and Mr and Mrs Hayashi.

 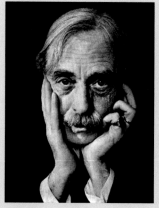 

Stéphane Mallarmé (left), Paul Valéry (centre) and Auguste Renoir (right) were among the friends and regular visitors whom Monet liked to welcome to Giverny.

The elegant Mrs Kuroki (née Princess Matsukata), Claude Monet, Lily Butler, Blanche Hoschedé-Monet and Georges Clemenceau photographed in the gardens at Giverny in 1921 by Mr Kuroki Sanji.

Monet's Bedroom: A Private Gallery

T his is the room in which Claude Monet died. There is nothing morbid about it, however. Clemenceau had rushed to his friend's deathbed, in a scene that has become legendary, replaying in real life the apocryphal anecdotes that have lent added colour to the lives of artists since the Renaissance, such as Leonardo da Vinci expiring in the arms of François I, as depicted notably by Ingres.

Lilla Cabot Perry, who wrote about her meetings with Monet in *The American Magazine of Art* in 1927, reported that his bedroom was 'a veritable gallery of Impressionist paintings' and described how he liked to linger over his Cézannes, adding that there was also a delightful painting by Berthe Morisot, the only woman in his world she had heard him give any praise, as she noted wryly.

As in the salon-studio, Hugues Gall called on the skills of Sylvie Patin and Hubert Le Gall in order to re-create an authentic hanging scheme – with the difference that here and in Monet's other private rooms, unlike in the large ground-floor room, no photographs survive to show them as they were during Monet's lifetime. Nevertheless, we do know which paintings he hung in these rooms, and it was therefore a simple matter to have good facsimiles made.

Monet displayed none of his own paintings in this part of the house, filling it instead with works by his friends, the young independent artists of the Impressionist era, as well as two works by Delacroix, which demonstrate the great romantic painter's fondness for painting en plein air and for seascapes painted from life. Arranged according to size on walls hung with white cloth, as in Monet's time, this reconstruction of Monet's private gallery does not suggest for a moment that visitors are viewing original paintings. But it allows them to enter inside both Monet's vision of the world and – in the most authentic fashion possible – his private domain.

The bed, simple and unadorned, is painted a pale colour. The rest of the furniture includes some very striking eighteenth-century pieces: a tombeau commode from the workshop of Louis Delaître, veneered in amaranth and with a top in grey-veined rouge royal marble, and a cylinder bureau in rosewood veneer, with bois violet inlays and a magnificent marquetry design featuring a musical score, a collector's piece stamped with the mark of the master cabinetmaker Nicolas Petit. Does the presence of these two outstanding pieces – so surprising in the bedroom of an artist who loved simplicity and was on the whole unmoved by opulence – testify to his love of the fine craftsmanship

Julie Manet, niece of Edouard Manet, described this room in 1893, 'with its big windows, pitch pine doors and floorboards and walls hung in white'. The white cloth with which the walls were hung set off a collection of works by Monet's friends, with Boudin, Caillebotte and Renoir among those whose images surrounded her as she slept.

of the Ancien Régime, as mentioned so often by his friend Renoir? Were they perhaps the last vestiges of the collections of Ernest Hoschedé from the chateau of Rottembourg, where Monet had been such a welcome guest? We can only speculate, as their provenance remains unknown.

The whole story of Impressionism is told on these walls, from its early beginnings to its later influence, from Monet's encounters with Boudin as a young artist and Renoir portraits of Monet and Camille in the passage outside to (to name only a few) a Renoir *Baigneuse*; two Cézannes that are now very famous, *Boy in a Red Waistcoat* and *Château Noir*; Caillebotte's *Paris Street; Rainy Day*; and a view of *Rouen Cathedral* by Signac.

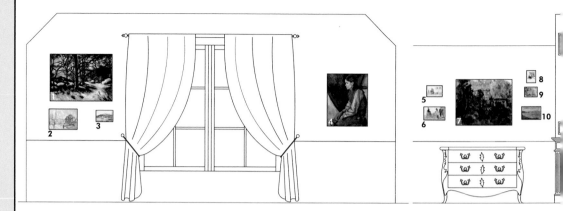

Bedroom

In the passage outside (not illustrated)
Paul Cézanne, *Portrait of Dominique Aubert*, c.1866, Winterthur, Am Römerholz, Oskar Reinhart Collection
Auguste Renoir, *Portrait of Claude Monet*, 1872, Paris, Musée Marmottan Monet, Michel Monet Bequest, 1966
Auguste Renoir, *Portrait of Camille Monet*, 1872, Paris, Musée Marmottan Monet, Michel Monet Bequest, 1966

To the left of the window
1. Paul Cézanne, *Melting Snow at Fontainebleau*, c.1880, New York, Museum of Modern Art
2. Paul Signac, *Rouen Cathedral*, Paris, Musée Marmottan Monet, Michel Monet Bequest, 1966
3. Johan Barthold Jongkind, *Port-Vendres*, 1880, Paris, Musée Marmottan Monet, Michel Monet Bequest, 1966

To the left of the fireplace
4. Paul Cézanne, *Boy in a Red Waistcoat*, 1888-90, New York, Museum of Modern Art
5. Eugène Boudin, *Fishing Boat on the Beach*, Paris, Musée Marmottan Monet, Michel Monet Bequest, 1966
6. Eugène Boudin, *Crinolines on the Beach*, Paris, Musée Marmottan Monet, Michel Monet Bequest, 1966
7. Paul Cézanne, *Château-Noir*, 1904-5, New York, Museum of Modern Art
8. Édouard Manet, *Head of a Man (Claude Monet)*, 1874, Paris, Musée Marmottan Monet,
   Michel Monet Bequest, 1966
9. Eugène Delacroix, *The Needle at Etretat*, Paris, Musée Marmottan Monet, Michel Monet Bequest, 1966
10. Eugène Delacroix, *Cliffs near Dieppe*, c.1852, Paris, Musée Marmottan Monet, Michel Monet Bequest, 1966

To the right of the fireplace
11. Berthe Morisot, *Julie Manet and her Greyhound Laertes*, 1893, Paris, Musée Marmottan Monet,
   Michel Monet Bequest, 1966
12. Berthe Morisot, *Young Girl with Basket*, 1891, Paris, Musée Marmottan Monet, Michel Monet Bequest, 1966

Above the bed
13. Auguste Renoir, *Bather seated on a Rock*, 1882, Paris, Musée Marmottan Monet, Michel Monet Bequest, 1966
14. Gustave Caillebotte, *Paris Street ; Rainy Day*, 1877, Paris, Musée Marmottan Monet,
   Michel Monet Bequest, 1966
15. Gustave Caillebotte, *White and Yellow Chrysanthemums, Garden at Petit Gennevilliers*, 1893, Paris, Musée
   Marmottan Monet, Michel Monet Bequest, 1966
16. Paul Cézanne, *Picnic on a Riverbank*, 1873-4, New Haven, Yale University Art Gallery
17. Eugène Boudin, *Boats and Fishermen*, Paris, Musée Marmottan Monet, Michel Monet Bequest, 1966
18. Johan Barthold Jongkind, *The Côte-Saint-André to Grand Lemps Road*, 1880, Paris, Musée Marmottan Monet,
   Michel Monet Bequest, 1966
19. Eugène Boudin, *Sailing Boats at Sea*, Paris, Musée Marmottan Monet, Michel Monet Bequest, 1966

To the right of the door
20. Gustave Caillebotte, *The Piano Lesson*, 1881, Paris, Musée Marmottan Monet, Michel Monet Bequest, 1966
21. Johan Barthold Jongkind, *Avignon*, 1873, Paris, Musée Marmottan Monet, Michel Monet Bequest, 1966

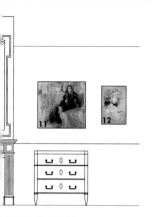
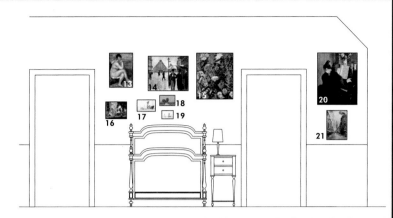

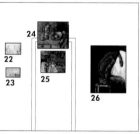
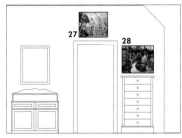

Bathroom

On the end wall

22. Paul Signac, *The Pont Valentré*, 1873, Paris, Musée Marmottan Monet, Michel Monet Bequest, 1966
23. Eugène Boudin, *On the Beach*, 1863, Paris, Musée Marmottan Monet, Michel Monet Bequest, 1966
24. Paul Cézanne, *Still Life with Milk Jug and Fruit*, c.1900, Washington, National Gallery of Art
25. Paul Cézanne, *Ginger Jar*, 1890-3, Washington, Phillips Collection
26. Paul Cézanne, *The Negro Scipio*, c.1867, São Paulo, Museu de Arte Assis Chateaubriand

Above the door

27. Paul Cézanne, *The Bathers*, c.1890-2, Saint Louis Art Museum

Above the chiffonnier

28. Paul Cézanne, *Turn in the Road*, 1881, Boston, Museum of Fine Arts

To the left of the window

29. Paul Signac, *Departure of Three-Masted Boats at Croix-de-Vie* (Vendée), Paris, Musée Marmottan Monet, Michel Monet Bequest, 1966
30. Paul Signac, *Venice, or The Gondolas*, 1908, Paris, Musée Marmottan Monet, Michel Monet Bequest, 1966

To the right of the window

31. Paul Cézanne, *L'Estaque*, 1879-1883, New York, Museum of Modern Art
32. Eugène Boudin, *St Catherine's Church, Honfleur*, c.1897, Honfleur, Musée Eugène-Boudin

The Bathroom: Paintings by Friends

Monet was proud of the Cézannes in his bathroom, as he made clear to Marc Elder: 'I have some admirable Cézannes upstairs, in particular a *Nègre* that's absolutely first class. That man thought about nothing but painting, loved nothing but painting ... And he never compromised!' And indeed this functional room houses two great masterpieces by Cézanne: *The Negro Scipio* (Museu de Arte, São Paulo) and *The Bathers* (Saint Louis Art Museum).

In choosing to hang these with a Jongkind from 1873 and a Signac from 1908, Monet seems to underline the enduring influence of the creative élan of the 1870s and the consistency of his own tastes. All the works in this part of the house speak first and foremost of friendship and companionship - paradoxically, he would have enjoyed them alone in these rooms, contemplating them with growing nostalgia, perhaps, as his friends from former times passed away.

42

Monet liked to show visitors his Cézannes – including some masterpieces displayed unceremoniously in his bathroom.

The first-floor rooms communicated with each other, so giving access directly from Alice's room to Claude's; the paintings in these rooms have been replaced with Japanese prints.

Alice's Bedroom and Bathroom

A number of paintings that were in the house in Monet's time have been hung here. A painting of an unknown child by Henri Frédéric Schopin (1804-1880) may be a family portrait. Two portraits by Adolphe Rinck (1802-1895) depict Monet's father Claude Adolphe Monet (1800-1871) and his mother, née Louise Justine Aubrée (1805-1857) in 1839, although nothing suggests that Monet's second wife would actually have had portraits of his parents – whom she never knew – in her bedroom. The very simple furniture has been drawn from elsewhere in the house, and the decorations are as close as possible to the schemes that would have been found in the private rooms of country houses in this region around 1900.

The furniture in Alice's room – consisting of pieces moved from elsewhere in the house and similar items from elsewhere – is typical of rural houses in Normandy at this time, and creates an authentic picture of daily life at Giverny around 1900.

Blanche's Bedroom:
The 'Blue Angel' and Monet's Favourite

Blanche's bedroom has also been refurnished, using the lilac shades in which it was decorated in Monet's time, with paintings hung as suggested in a rediscovered sketch that Blanche herself made of her room. Some of the furniture now in the room was found stored in the attic. On the walls are a *Haystack* by Blanche and a painting by Lucien Pissaro (son of Camille), and in the little sewing room between Blanche's room and her mother's hangs an oil painting by Lilla Cabot Perry, *Alice in the Lane*. Family photographs help to conjure up the private world of Monet's favourite daughter-in-law.

The decorations in Blanche's bedroom are predominantly in mauve tones. Blanche loved to paint: above the secretaire hangs one of the images of haystacks that she painted on trips into the countryside with Monet.

Blanche – Monet's stepdaughter by his marriage to Alice, and his daughter-in-law by her own marriage to his son Jean – was confident enough to become a painter in the great man's shadow, and without being his pupil in the strict sense of the term used to accompany him on his painting trips into the country.

Monet's Two Gardens

When Gerald Van der Kemp embarked on the restoration of Monet's garden, all that remained was rough grass infested with weeds. The lily pond had turned into a bog. There were no surviving plans from the time when it was created to serve as references for an identical reconstruction of the garden, which – to add to all these difficulties – was forever in a state of flux, as Monet constantly introduced new improvements and embellishments. Records of seed orders found in the archives and Monet's many paintings of the garden have therefore served as references for an idealized version of Giverny, in which (as Oscar Wilde observed) life imitates art. Faithful as it is in every respect to Monet's paintings, the garden today clearly cannot be a faithful copy of the garden as Monet knew it, if only because it is open to the public for several months of the year, and every visitor – particularly those for whom this is the visit of a lifetime – must see it at its best. And the devoted garden lovers who come back again and again in order to enjoy every planting scheme and flowering season as they unfold, as the hundreds of plants raised under glass are planted out, must also be satisfied.

Visitors today may therefore share the same sensations as those who came to see Monet. There is no geometrical centre to these gardens: you need to simply lose yourself in them, letting your gaze wander over drifts of iris, nasturtiums and roses and glide over the water lilies as they are reflected in the surface of the water through the seasons. With its multiple vantage points, the kaleidoscopic, ever-changing world of the gardens echoes that of the house where so many of Monet's paintings hang. From the initial straight paths to the sinuous walks around the lake, from the vantage point of the verandah hugging the house to the panoramas from the Japanese bridge and the little footbridge, Monet set out to create a succession of moving images.

Viewed through one of the windows, the flower beds of the Clos Normand still have a traditional, conventional air, offering no hint of the presence beyond the shrubs at the far end of the water garden, with its rushes and reeds, bamboos and water lilies.

The Clos Normand: Former Orchard and First Garden

Nothing could be further removed from the flower panels Monet painted for the salon doors of his art dealer friend Paul Durand-Ruel – well-mannered decorative pieces designed to complement the most classically bourgeois of interiors, for which he had already painted chrysanthemums on three occasions – and the final explosion of the paintings that Monet called his 'grandes décorations' and that together formed the Water Lilies cycle.

Monet was familiar with the large and beautiful gardens of his friend Caillebotte at Yerres (now open to the public), and of Ernest Hoschedé, Alice's then husband and his friend, on his splendid estate at the chateau of Rottembourg at Montgeron. On his travels he always visited gardens, from Hyde Park to Bordighera, but his interest at this stage was more conventional than botanical, and he was content to conform to the horticultural fashions of the age. It was during the difficult years he spent at Argenteuil that he developed a deeper interest in plants and gardening.

In this first garden at Giverny, Monet opened up the view to the horizon and felled the sombre trees that might cast too much shade (including some conifers to which Alice was attached), retaining only a pair of yews flanking the start of the sandy walk. The rest – at a time when informal gardens à l'anglaise had long been the vogue – was laid out on a geometrical plan, with a small, simplified version designed by himself of a formal garden à la française, structured by right-angled beds. The flower beds edged with irises, one of his favourite flowers, exemplified the Monet style of flower gardening, with squares of different colours carefully aligned like paintings on a wall. Perennials dominated his schemes, with annuals mixed in among them, without any particular interest – with the exception of the dahlias and orchids that were all the rage – in exotic or rare species.

On pergolas, gates and the house façade, meanwhile, Monet grew a wealth of roses, mingling the choicest species with wild eglantines. In order to appreciate the effect of these single-colour plantings, laid out side by side as though on a palette, a variety of points of view had to be arranged, with due regard not only for the squares but also for the diagonals, which at a stroke mixed up all the different colours as an artist mixes paints. This was a garden planted as a place to paint in, an open-air studio. Monet liked to work in the surrounding countryside, painting haystacks and rows of poplars – the Fondation Claude-Monet has bought one of the fields in which he painted in order to preserve it – and in his garden he was as close as he could be to the colours and subjects that he loved. When he was away from this little world that he had created, he was sometimes

In the seventeenth century, tulip mania led to wild speculation on the prized bulbs, which were already a major inspiration for artists. In Monet's time they came back into fashion once more, and he loved to create effects with them, using the full spectrum of colours available from specialist nurseries, from yellow to black.

A Garage
for a Magnificent Motorcar

The small building that housed the second studio (and now houses the administrative offices), opposite the glasshouses, also contained a garage on its ground floor. Now used by technical services and not open to the public, in Monet's time this was a place of some importance.

Fascinated by technical advances, like all the men of his generation, in 1901 Monet treated himself to a gleaming new Panhard & Levassor motorcar, right-hand drive, with two seats front and back and a leather interior, a sumptuous salon on wheels in which he drove round the countryside, to the great astonishment of the local populace. His driver, Sylvain, was the son of a groom who was incorrigibly nostalgic for the traditional hunts for which his father had worked in the Sologne. In the evening he would sound his hunting horn to amuse the children, and in the daytime he was a proper chauffeur, complete with cap and goggles. Short drives to Gaillon or Lamotte-Beuvron, perhaps to sample the new recipe for apple tart invented by the Tatin sisters, were punctuated by longer adventures, such as the trip to the Spanish border in 1904, where Monet caught the train to go to Madrid and the Prado.

In his keen interest in technical advances and inventions, Monet was a man of his time. He also displayed a certain taste for luxury when he bought a Panhard motorcar, in which he went for long drives through the surrounding countryside. This photograph shows him with his son-in-law Theodore Butler in around 1910.

seized by what he described in his letters to Alice as 'melancholy for Giverny'. He often sent her very precise instructions: 'Tell me if the chrysanthemums I sowed are in flower; if so and if some of them are pretty, mark them with a length of wool.' From Belle-Ile, in 1892, he sent her gardening tips, highlighted by Sylvie Patin as an indication that this was the point at which he turned from painting still lifes to depicting living nature: 'Thank you for taking such care over my precious flowers, you are a good gardener; it's not urgent yet to dig up the gladioli, but when you do I recommend planting perennials, anemones and my pretty clematis.' He had become an expert gardener, with a passion for tulips: in 1886 he went to the Dutch tulip fields to paint them, concluding that the sight was 'marvellous, but enough to drive a poor painter mad'. Chrysanthemums had not yet acquired the funereal associations that they have had since 1918 in France and some other countries. They were one of Monet's favourite flowers imported from Japan, a link between the Clos Normand, which was no longer exclusively devoted to plants found in Normandy, and the print collection inside the house.

Monet was thus constantly going to and fro between a garden-studio, where he loved to paint from nature whenever the weather permitted, and his indoor studios, to which he never withdrew without grumbling but where he got work done nonetheless, inspired by the nature that was so close to create true plein-air effects. In an article published in *Le Figaro* in 1907, Marcel Proust wrote of Giverny, where he had never been. Drawing on others' descriptions of the place and his own observations of Monet's paintings, he offered an extraordinarily compelling and perceptive analysis of the relationship between art and nature: 'There I shall see, in a garden of tones and colours more even than of flowers, a garden that must be not so much a flower garden as a colour garden, as one might call it, flowers arranged to form a whole that is not quite as it would be in nature, since they have been sown in such a way as to ensure that only matching shades will be in bloom at any one time, forming an infinity of harmonies in drifts of blues or pinks, and somehow dematerialized, by this powerfully manifested painterly will, of everything but their colour. Not only garden flowers but also aquatic blooms, the delicate water lilies that the master has depicted in sublime compositions for which this garden (a true transposition of art even more than a subject for paintings, a painting that has already been created through nature and that is lit up by the gaze of a great artist) is like a preliminary sketch in living form.'

Proust was the first to realize that Giverny was far more than the sum of its parts. He understood that this was no longer merely a fashionable flower garden filled with rare species; instead it had risen to the condition of painting, becoming a 'transposition of art'.

Monet loved flowers in clear, pure tones, letting them spread and self-seed to create the pools of saturated colour that can also be found in some of his paintings.

Tulips add the first splashes of colour in spring, combining with daffodils and narcissi, wallflowers and forget-me-nots to create compositions that are still contained by the flowerbeds and do not yet spill over on to the paths. The plays of light filtering between the dark branches of the pair of yew trees create unexpected effects that Monet loved to watch. Perpetually in movement and ever changing, the garden offered a constant spectacle of unpredictable images and effects.

Octave Mirbeau, Writer among the Flowers at Giverny

In 1891, Octave Mirbeau (1848-1917) – writer, art lover, keen botanist and close friend of Monet – composed a prose poem brimming with sensual descriptions of the colours and perfumes of the flowers he had seen blooming in his friend's garden as the seasons unfolded, combining an eroticization of the garden with impeccable botanical accuracy.

'Spring arrives.

The wallflowers exhale their final fragrances; the peonies, the divine peonies, have faded; the hyacinths are dead. Already the nasturtiums are showing their young leaves tinged with bronze and the California poppies their delicious lime green fronds; and edging the broad flowerbeds against a backdrop of flower meadows, irises unfold the strange curves of their petals, frilled with white, mauve, lilac, yellow and blue, streaked with shades of brown and smudges of purple, with the complex structure of their undersides evoking enigmatic analogies, musings as alluring and depraved as those that hover around the disturbing blooms of orchids…

Summer arrives.

In the broad flowerbeds, over the deadheaded irises, surges a magical and astonishing wave of poppies; an extraordinary mingling of tones, an orgy of pale tones, a magnificent and melodic confusion of white, pink, yellow and mauve; an incredible lineation of blonde flesh tones against which orange shades dazzle, glowing coppers trumpet their fanfares, reds bleed and flame, violets cheer and deep purples blaze. And here and there, emerging from these glorious waves, from this glorious river of flowers, hollyhocks raise their spikes of exquisitely rumpled, filmy blooms, light and gauzy, their folds glistening and satin-smooth, their trumpets billowing and ballooning like tiny tutus. And the Texas sunflowers stretch out their long bracts swelling with buds, and the California sunflowers soar upwards, shooting out their green eyes, fringing their tousled blooms with gold, like fabulous bickering birds. And on the breeze floats the cool breath of all the rest, mingling with the peppery notes of the nasturtiums.

Autumn arrives.

After the magical spectacle of the poppies comes the sumptuous display of the dahlias; fluted ruffs, delicately edged with fine gold, crimsons red as blood, melting lilacs; double pompoms, vividly brilliant or discreetly nuanced; stars that tremble and shimmer on slender branching stems, charming in their bold, blithe grace; or shreds of antique silk, subdued in tone and with deliciously faded embroideries; or enormous plumes with jagged petals fray, spread, twist themselves in flowing crimson manes. [...] The gladioli, latecomers as ever, proffer their opulent calyces and lily-like throats to the love-struck flight of bees. And in the breeze filled with all these reflections, frissons and pollens, the dizzy sunflowers turn their yellow discs, shining and blazing, and the tall harpaliums scatter a constant and never-ending stream of gold blooms.

[...]

It is here, among this ever-unfolding feast for the eyes, that Claude Monet lives. And it is just the setting that we might imagine for this prodigious painter of the splendours of colour, for this prodigious poet of soft light and veiled forms, for the painter of compositions that you can breathe, filled with fragrance and intoxication; who was able to touch the untouchable, to express the inexpressible; and who cast a spell over our dreams with all the dreams that nature mysteriously enfolds, with all the dreams with which the divine light is mysteriously sprinkled.'

Claude Monet, *The Artist's Garden at Giverny*, 1900, Paris, musée d'Orsay.

The composition of this painting demonstrates how Monet used the effects that he had created in his garden, with verticals in darker tones, diagonals cutting across the rectangular arrangement of the beds, and the mirror-like echoes of the blooms in the foreground, almost as though they are reflected in water. Saturated with colour, the composition would be almost abstract were it not for the glimpses of the house in the background..

After the spectacular displays of spring bulbs and fruit trees
in blossom, the roses and clematis that festoon the arches
and trellises help to continue the impression of abundance –
with flowers spilling over every surface, both horizontal and
vertical – that Monet also sought to create in his paintings.

He was the first to intuit the journey towards abstraction that Giverny had undergone – its flowers being 'dematerialized' – and the metamorphosis, difficult to believe at this period, of a fragment of nature into a work of art. Did Monet read these lines by the writer who six years later would publish the first volume of *In Search of Lost Time*, another example of a total work of art? During the war that started seven years later, the 'delicate water lilies' would be transformed into a solitary struggle within the space of the canvas: an artist's struggle against the darkness that was overwhelming him and the barbarism that surrounded him, isolated – like Proust in his sick room – in the midst of a world that he was striving to re-create.

A path on the left, as you stand with your back to the house, leads past the henhouse to the *Water Lilies* studio. When on one occasion Alice announced (to Marc Elder's amusement) that 'the little Japanese have flown', it transpired that she was referring to some Japanese hens that had escaped. 'They matter to me,' was Monet's response, 'they were a present from Clemenceau.' Happily they were found.

At the far end of the Clos Normand, on the right hand side, are the glasshouses – Monet was at pains to ensure that the stove in his hothouse was always well stoked – and the small building that was Monet's second studio and is now home to the administrative offices of the Fondation Claude-Monet. It also houses Monet's library. Far from being a bibliophile's collection of rare volumes, the scope of the works here bears witness to Monet's cultivated and literary tastes. Horticultural reviews rub shoulders with literary works by his contemporaries: to the end of his life, Monet was a great reader. Henry Vidal later remembered that at his funeral an edition of Baudelaire's poems lay on a table in the studio, its pages open at '*L'Etranger*' ('The Stranger'), with its concluding lines:
'*J'aime les nuages... les nuages qui passent... là-bas... là-bas... les merveilleux nuages!*'
'I love the clouds ... the clouds that pass ... yonder ... yonder ... the marvellous clouds!'.

Behind the gate lies the road that runs between the Clos Normand and the water garden, which visitors now cross through an underpass.

Overleaf: In late summer the garden is a mass of luxuriant profusion, the central path is submerged by drifts of nasturtiums, and the shapes of the flowerbeds are blurred with colour, like a painting flowing out over the confines of its frame – an effect that Monet was to create when he abandoned traditional easel painting in order to create his *Water Lilies*.

Sacha Guitry, from Film to Reportage

In 1915, Sacha Guitry had the inspired idea of filming a galaxy of distinguished figures, from Anatole France to Rodin, at work. He spotted Degas, who refused to take part, on a Paris boulevard; he travelled to Provence to see Renoir at Les Collettes; and he went to Giverny to see Monet. His private gallery in his Paris residence on avenue Elisée-Reclus featured in place of honour a circular painting from the *Water Lilies* cycle, as well as a smaller landscape painting, *Gust of Wind on the Loire*. The film is silent, and as Monet is shown at a distance, or shaded by his hat and talking into his beard, it is impossible to decipher what he is saying in this unique and poignant document. Monet liked photographers, and was perfectly at ease with the young Guitry, posing in his white suit and straw hat, painting at his easel under a large light-coloured parasol beside the lily pond, smoking a cigarette with his dog beside him. When Guitry asked Monet if he would give him one of his brushes, selecting the oldest one he could find, Monet offered him a new one, protesting 'at least it will be useful'. In 1952, Guitry added his own commentary to these silent images of his heroes, recorded in his study, to make a film entitled *Ceux de chez nous*. It was to prove a great success.

Monet and his Gardeners

At Giverny, Monet's passion for gardening assumed impressive proportions, as he ordered hundreds of sacks of seed and topsoil to improve the chalky soil along the banks of the Seine. It appears to have been his friend and accomplice Georges Truffaut (1872-1948), descended from a long line of gardeners stretching back to the sixteenth century, who came up with the name 'Clos Normand' for this hectare of land. Monet set about transforming it by felling the conifers that grew there and erecting trelliswork arches to span the length of the path leading to the house from the road. Monet alternated between the two garden suppliers Truffaut and Vilmorin – both still in existence today – for his deliveries of seeds, bulbs and shrubs, and ordered his water lilies from the Latour-Marliac nursery, which had made them a speciality.

In its early, slightly homespun state, Monet's garden was an ideal playground for the children. But as its structure became more intricate, he began to be increasingly concerned with creating flowering timetables that would extend colour in the garden over several months and create skilful harmonies. To this end he decided to employ a proper head gardener, took out a subscription to *Country Life*, the elegant magazine for garden-lovers, and invested in horticultural dictionaries and plant catalogues. Félix Breuil, who came with a recommendation from Octave Mirbeau's father, was the first gardener at Giverny, where he found himself subject to the whims of an artist who in the field of plants and flowers now boasted all the authority of the self-taught expert. He was succeeded by Louis Lebret, who after Monet's death stayed on as gardener for Blanche. Working under them was a team of five under-gardeners, who also looked after the water garden and water lilies. When Gérald Van der Kemp embarked on his restoration of the garden, the head gardener was Gilbert Vahé, a graduate of the Ecole d'Horticulture de Versailles, who was also devoted to archive research. His approach was that of a historian and archeologist, as well as an artist. Today, the gardens are overseen by James Priest.

A number of autochrome images of the gardens are a useful aid to today's gardeners, who every year create a fresh version of 'Monet's garden', based partly on painstaking reconstruction and partly on sensitive interpretation. Restoring a garden is a very different matter from restoring a historic building.

Claude Monet in 1889, six years after he moved to Giverny, photographed by Theodore Robinson.

Claude Monet at Giverny in the spring of 1921, by an unknown photographer.

The Water Garden: A Monet Masterpiece

An underpass, built thanks to the generosity of Ambassador and Mrs Walter Annenberg, now enables visitors to reach the water garden without crossing the road. In Monet's time the railway ran along the old 'chemin du Roy', bringing an element of modernity to the landscape that was far from unwelcome to the painter of the Gare Saint-Lazare.

Clemenceau tesitified to the importance of the water garden in Monet's daily routine: 'The idea of the *Water Lilies* laid hold of Monet over a long period. Every morning he would spend hours beside his pond, watching in silence as the clouds and patches of blue sky passed in magical procession over his *"garden of water and fire"*.' This was evidently Monet's own description of the world apart that he had constructed around his pond by diverting a branch of the River Epte. After overcoming the objections of landowners along the riverbanks, who feared seeing 'their' water poisoned by exotic plant species, he had been obliged to seek special permission from the prefect of the department. From his conversations with Monet, Clemenceau understood the dual nature of this spot. Conceived first and foremost as an aid to Monet's art, another 'picturesque' subject for his paintings, it had gradually come to take its place; in parallel, meanwhile, in the large modern studio just a few paces away, a vision of water and fire was taking shape that no longer needed to be painted 'from life', and that was on the path to abstraction.

Clemenceau went on: 'Monet's garden was one of his works, a realization of the charms of adapting nature to the work of the painter of light.' The reversal was clear: after centuries of the mimetic tradition, here art dared to go beyond the imitation of nature; here, nature was moulded to the artist's conception of it. For Gérald Van der Kemp – who had restored Versailles, another example of a total work of art where, as Saint-Simon put it, the king had 'taken nature by force' – this close association was of paramount importance. At Versailles, as Philippe Beaussant has pointed out in *Louis XIV artiste*, visitors enter into a work of art, in an experience that adds a compelling extra dimension to what might otherwise be simply a visit to a palace and its gardens. Similarly, the key to the restoration of Giverny – and to its care to this day – lies in viewing it as a work of art in its own right. It was here, beside the Japanese bridge, that Monet confided to Marc Elder: 'It took me a while to understand my water lilies. I had planted them for pleasure; I grew them without thinking of painting of them ... You don't absorb a landscape in a single day ...

This second garden was far more than a mere concession to the vogue for all things Japanese at this period. Monet had seen photographs of water gardens in Java, possibly brought back by his friend Clemenceau, and wanted to create a world apart, a world that would be his alone. Here all was meandering and sinuous, with a subtle play between the horizontal surfaces of the water lilies and the vertical lines of the gorse and willow fronds.

Clemenceau at Giverny

The friendship between Claude Monet and Georges Clemenceau was a long one, stretching way back to the 1860s, when Clemenceau was just a medical student with an interest in politics and Monet a penniless young artist. Monet followed all the vicissitudes of the political career of the great radical statesman and war leader, who was also a major art-lover and collector. Their friendship, founded on a shared opposition to the repressive policies of the Second Empire and championing of Alfred Dreyfus until his innocence was eventually established, became increasingly important to both men as the years went by.

Monet sent Clemenceau his *Study of Rocks (Le Bloc)* painted in the Creuse, as a symbol of the fight for 'right and truth'. Touched by this gesture, Clemenceau hung the painting in his study and wrote to Monet: 'Thanking you would be as idiotic as thanking a shaft of sunlight.' But Clemenceau was not just a great friend and fellow champion, like Monet's other friend Zola, of advanced ideas: he was also a keen gardener, who was struggling to make a garden on sandy soil overlooking the sea in the Vendée, and who made frequent visits to Giverny to seek Monet's advice. When he saw that his old friend's eyesight was beginning to fail, he remembered his medical training and examined him. In the wake of the Great War, this heroic friend who was now dubbed 'Père la Victoire' (Father Victory) took advantage of his first free day, just a week after the signature of the Armistice on 11 November 1918, to pay a visit to Giverny. In 1926, when Monet was eighty-six and close to death, he rushed to his friend's bedside. Monet died in his arms.

Clemenceau played a central part in the lengthy negotiations that were to lead to the installation of the *Water Lilies* paintings in the Orangerie. In 1927, he presided over the inauguration of the paintings, a gift from Monet to a France battered and bruised by war. In his moving last letter to his friend, Clemenceau wrote: 'I'm as mad as you are, but my madness is different from yours. This is why we will always understand each other so well.'

Claude Monet with his old friend Georges Clemenceau on the Japanese bridge, 1921.

The bridge offered not only a vantage point in the heart of this natural profusion, but also an ideal setting for photographs of Monet and his distinguished friends.

72

As well as creating a network of vertical lines, the bamboos also form a shady area in the water garden, with deeper tones making dark reflections of the stream that Monet had diverted. Planted, shaped and designed like a great painting, this 'natural' idyll is in fact an entirely man-made masterpiece.

Then suddenly I had a revelation, and I saw all the enchantments of my pond. I took up my palette ... Since then I've hardly painted anything else.' The way Monet describes this passionate coup de foudre is striking: it was only gradually, and without any preconceived notions on his part, that the garden became a work of art. There were parallels here with the process by which the group of disparate and ill-assorted young artists who exhibited at the Salon des Indépendants in 1874 invented – spontaneously and without any predetermined manifesto – the movement that was to become known to the world as Impressionsim.

Claude Monet, *The Water Lily Pond, Green Harmony*, 1899, Paris, musée d'Orsay.

The musical sense of the word 'harmony', as in the title of this painting, is one of the keys to understanding this garden, which Monet designed like a piece of music. In 1905, Claude Debussy would compose the first of his suites of *Images*, entitled *Reflections in the Water*.

Overleaf: Claude Monet, *Water Lilies, Evening Effect*, 1897-8, Paris, musée Marmottan Monet.

The wisterias, white and purple, festoon the bridge just as roses clothe the arches over the central path. Standing on his Japanese bridge, Monet was at the heart of the world he had created, surrounded by colour and suffused with light. The critic Arsène Alexandre spoke of a 'large studio planted in the midst of a flower-filled bog garden, like a tent and an observatory', the bridge having itself become the main subject of several series of paintings.

The *Water Lilies* Studio, Monet's Last Refuge

This large building was constructed at the height of the First World War, thanks to special permissions that clearly testify to Monet's prestige as France's greatest living painter. Both his earlier studios had been lit, in the nineteenth-century tradition, by tall vertical windows, as in Bazille's painting of *The Artist's Studio, Rue de la Condamine* (1869-70, Musée d'Orsay). This third studio, however, was endowed with the top-lighting preferred by a new generation of artists, who had started their careers working in garrets lit by skylights. This was the first major studio of the twentieth century, and the way in which the *Water Lilies* are now displayed at the Orangerie replicates this essential feature. In Monet's time, the 'brutalism' of the décor was relieved by a handsome wooden floor, which he took care to protect from paint splashes as he worked. The house and gardens at Giverny are a world of illusions, a world that owes nothing to nature, but that was created by an artist for his art. In this space the absence of nature reaches its ultimate expression: here, in this first laboratory of abstraction, all is reduced to light.

As reports of battles and casualty lists reached Giverny and every other village in France, this studio was witness to a struggle of a different kind. The austerity of this empty space and the rigour of its architecture cannot be understood in isolation from the war. 'I wanted to shut myself away on my own,' Monet explained, 'to lose myself in work so as not to think any more about all the horrors being committed so relentlessly ... I lived there for five or six years, hardly putting my brush down ...'

Today the building houses the shop and bookshop where visitors can browse a large selection of titles principally about Monet, from scholarly works to books for children. Monet, for whom this modern shed served a strictly functional purpose, would doubtless have approved. The shop offers a wide range of carefully selected souvenirs, from silk scarves to Limoges porcelain – Limoges still produces the white plates with a yellow border edged with blue that were used at Giverny. Visitors can also buy replicas of the Creil faience service with a blue Japanese-inspired motif, as well as cider, preserves and other organic produce supplied by local farms, just as in Monet's time.

The profusion of the garden and the saturation of the space are even more evident in late summer: engulfed in this world of lush greenery, the bridge and landing stage become merely incidental. In Monet's paintings, too, the subject gradually vanished, leaving colour and light triumphant.

Monet wanted to merge the water lily pads, floating on the surface of the water, with the reflections of overhanging branches. What exactly are we looking at in these reflections punctuated with small splashes of red? This superimposing of surfaces on the flatness of the pond recalls the similar layering of paint in his last work, the *Water Lilies* paintings. The world that awaits the visitor at the Orangerie – a world that is closed in on itself but open to the imagination – similarly stands outside both time and space.

From the *Water Lilies* Studio to the Orangerie

Claude Monet, *Water Lilies: Morning* (1920-1926), detail, Paris, musée de l'Orangerie.

When the *Water Lilies* series was unveiled to the public at the Orangerie it received a muted reception – a major disappointment to Clemenceau, whose initiative this had been after his friend's death. Not until after the Second World War, when American artists in Paris grasped the major significance of this break from all that had gone before, including Impressionism, was their growing success assured. These galleries devoted to a work of seminal importance to twentieth-century art, accessible to all, are today a place of pilgrimage, like the gardens at Giverny. Both are now places of contemplation and meditation for large numbers of visitors, including many artists, who appreciate the indissoluble links between the gardens, changing with the months and shifting with the winds, and the space created by the paintings.

Monet, photographed here in his last studio at Giverny, with its modern metal structure, could not bring himself to part with his last paintings, which he had bequeathed to the French nation. It fell to his friend Clemenceau, after his death, to inaugurate the *Water Lilies* paintings at the Orangerie, between the gardens of the Louvre, haunted by the shades of past painters, and the Seine, the vital inspiration of both Monet's life and his work.

The *Water Lilies* Studio at Giverny.

CLAUDE MONET: FROM NORMANDY TO JAPAN

SAVING MONET'S HOUSE

Gérald Van der Kemp had provided the impetus necessary to save Versailles: charismatic and charming, he impressed patrons with both his conversation and his lofty presence, as he revealed the palace and gardens to them in a new light. Still full of energy after his retirement, he was entrusted – as a member of the Académie des Beaux-Arts – with the directorship of Giverny. There he applied to the garden – in a way that proved quite outstanding – the major principles of restoration that he had elaborated for the reconstruction of the bedchambers of Louis XIV and Marie Antoinette. Authentic species of plants and flowers had to be tracked down, exactly as though they were historic pieces of furniture or antique silk hangings. After the initial phase of work to save the site – a colossal operation – he had time only to carry out a general refurbishment of the house, including the restoration of its orginal colour schemes. The work he initiated continues to this day.

The major patrons who made it possible to save the house from damp and the gardens from neglect were notably members of the 'Versailles Foundation, Inc./Claude Monet-Giverny', presided over by Florence Van der Kemp, who was responsible for raising so many gifts from American donors, as well as M. and Mme Michel David-Weill for the restoration of the prints, furniture and large *Water Lilies* studio. The Conseil Général de l'Eure made the restoration of the gardens possible. The restoration of the neighbouring Duboc farmhouse, which offers accommodation to artists, was made possible by patrons including notably Lila Acheson Wallace (Reader's Digest Fund), the Florence J. Gould Foundation, Mr and Mrs Laurance S. Rockefeller, Baron Edmond de Rothschild, the Princess Grace of Monaco Foundation, Beatriz Patiño, the interior designer Henri Samuel, and the actress and great art collector Jacqueline Delubac, who had been married to Sacha Guitry. A plaque in the entrance hall lists all these benefactors who have thus written a chapter in the history of Giverny.

It was during Gérald Van der Kemp's tenure that Giverny became famous. Since that time the popularity of Monet's house and garden has continued to grow, and distinguished visitors have included Empress Farah of Iran, Princess Grace of Monaco and more recently Hillary Clinton. Other notable American and Japanese names have further enlarged the circle of loyal benefactors and patrons who have played their part in the story of the saving of Monet's house.

In Monet's Footsteps: Through the Village

In Monet's time the village numbered some three hundred inhabitants; today the population is no more than five hundred, and the village is very well preserved. The 'chemin du Roy', which Louis IX (St Louis) would have taken to visit his mother Blanche of Castile in the thirteenth century, bisects the village, with magnificent views over the surrounding countryside. The little railway line was once a useful amenity and added a touch of modern industrialism that was appreciated by the Impressionists.

Today little has changed. The Romanesque church of Ste Radegonde, classified as a historic monument, is surrounded by a poignant graveyard containing on one side the graves of the Monet-Hoschedé family – the discreet marble plaque bearing the dates of Claude Monet is especially moving – and nearby the graves of Gérald and Florence Van der Kemp. A handsome bronze medallion depicts Van der Kemp in patrician profile and wearing his academician's robes, while the sun behind him symbolizes his two great – and inimitably French – passions, Versailles in the time of

*'I am in raptures,
the countryside of Giverny is glorious for me.'*

Louis XIV and the light of the Impressionists. Other monuments close by commemorate airmen killed during the Second World War. The memorial to local men who fell in the First World War bears the names of farmers who were Monet's neighbours, such as Fernand Duboc. Thirteen men from Giverny were killed in the war, as the aged Monet fought his own battle in his studio to make a gift to his country and to Clemenceau of his monument to victory and act of faith in universal peace, the *Water Lilies*. An antique hearse inside the church might be the same one that brought Monet to his last resting place, when Clemenceau swept off the black undertaker's cloth covering the coffin, declaring, 'No black for Monet.' The harmonium was a gift to the church from Monet's son-in-law Theodore Butler.

In the village, the old Hôtel Baudy, opened in 1887 by Lucien and Angélina Baudy, who were followed by their son Gaston and his wife Clarisse in 1896, repays a visit for the sake of its interior, largely unchanged since the time when friends who came to visit Monet stayed there when there was no room in the house. Reached through the very 1890s dining room is the garden, filled with old roses, at the bottom of which stands the studio used by the colony of American artists who surrounded Monet. Built in 1887, the studio was the first to be built in the village, and remains as it was when Cézanne, Rodin, Sisley and Mary Cassatt worked in it, as well as all the young American artists who came before 1914.

Today many artists still come to stay in Giverny in order to experience the light that Monet knew, in this 'village of painters'.

THE MUSÉE DES IMPRESSIONISMES AT GIVERNY

In 2009, this modern building, designed by the architectural firm of Reichen et Robert as the 'American art museum' in Giverny and run by the Terra Foundation for American Art (named after the great collector and patron Daniel Terra), became a museum of 'Impressionisms', displaying work by artists from throughout the world in addition to those from America. The local community groups who have taken over the running of the museum have been able, thanks to gifts and loans, to put together the kernel of a permanent Impressionist collection around the works of Claude Monet. Many talks and other events on artistic themes are held in the auditorium.

Kitagawa: Monet's Garden in Japan

Although he was unable to see through the project himself, the idea of building a copy of Giverny in Japan – a country where historic monuments form an important part of the national heritage – was dear to Gérald Van der Kemp and his Japanese friends. In 1999, a version of the central section of the house at Giverny and above all the garden, with its arches evoking the Clos Normand, was created in the Japanese spa town of Kitigawa. The flowers and blooming periods may not correspond exactly, but the magic is nonetheless present, and frequent exchanges take place between the gardeners at Kitagawa and at Giverny. In a sense, the gardens at Kitagawa are also 'Monet's garden', for if Monet never went to the Land of the Rising Sun he certainly dreamed of doing so. This little piece of Giverny in Japan has proved a great success.

Monet in Normandy

Every year in Honfleur, Le Havre, Caen, Rouen and Saint-Lô, the museums of Normandy participate in a shared venture, attracting large numbers of visitors to local festivals and exhibitions. The Impressionist painters loved Normandy, and the region's museums, especially Rouen, possess many works of interest. The places that played a significant part in Impressionism are also the landscapes that inspired Monet: the cottage at Varengeville, Honfleur, Le Havre, Sainte-Adresse, Trouville and of course Etretat, with its beach, its cliffs and its famous 'needle'.

Claude Monet, Impressionism, Normandy and Giverny

1840
14 November, birth of Claude Monet in Paris.

c.1845
The Monet family moves to Le Havre in Normandy.

c.1856-7
Monet exhibits his first caricatures.

1859-60
He goes to Paris, where he enrols in the Académie Suisse (named after its founder) and meets Pissarro.

1861
Monet does his military service in Algeria, where he discovers Mediterranean skies and nature.

1862
At Gleyre's studio Monet meets Bazille, Renoir and probably Sisley, the first group of young artists to dream of bringing about major changes in art.

1864
In a significant meeting, Monet works alongside Boudin.

1865
Monet sends his first landscapes to the Salon, the official art exhibition.

1866
He exhibits *Camille* at the Salon, a portrait of his first partner, Camille Doncieux. Meets Edouard Manet.

1867
Birth of Jean, Monet and Camille's first son.

1869-70
Monet endures rejections by the Salon and marries Camille. The Franco-Prussian War breaks out; Bazille is killed in action.

1870-1
With Pissarro, Monet discovers London. Meets the art dealer Paul Durand-Ruel, an encounter of decisive importance.

1871-2
Monet works at Argenteuil, where he begins to take a real interest in gardening.

1874
The exhibition *Impression, Sunrise* (Musée Marmottan-Monet) at Nadar's studio gives Impressionism its name.

Monet photographed at the entrance to his second studio by his friend Baron de Meyer, 1905 (private collection).

1876

Second Impressionism exhibition. Monet paints in the gardens à *l'anglaise* of the Château de Rottembourg at Montgeron, home of his friends and loyal supporters Alice and Ernest Hoschedé.

1877

At the third Impressionist exhibition, Monet appears first and foremost as a painter of the modern world with his views of the Gare Saint-Lazare, departure point of trains for Normandy.

1878

Birth of Michel, second son of Camille and Claude. The family leaves Paris and moves to Vétheuil.

1879

Fourth Impressionist exhibition, at which Monet shows twenty-nine canvases. Death of Camille.

1880

Fifth Impressionist exhibition. Monet exhibits at the Salon.

1881

Monet sets up home with Alice Hoschedé and the children at the Villa Saint-Louis in Poissy.

1882

Seventh Impressionist exhibition, Monet shows thirty-five works.

1883

After a return to Le Havre and a stay in Etretat, in April Monet and Alice Hoschedé become tenants at Giverny.

1885

Monet returns several times to the coast at Etretat. Forms a friendship with Guy de Maupassant.

1886

In New York, Durand-Ruel mounts an exhibition of the 'Paris Impressionists', including forty paintings by Monet.

1887

Monet returns to London, where he exhibits at the Royal Society of British Artists in November.

1888

Trips to Antibes and Juan-les-Pins and to London.

1889

Trip to the Creuse. Monet launches a subscription to buy Manet's *Olympia* for the nation.

1890

Monet buys Giverny and embarks on works there, building a second studio and transforming the garden.

1891

Durand-Ruel exhibits the *Haystack* paintings.

1892

Durand-Ruel exhibits the *Poplars* paintings.
Monet stays in Rouen and paints his *Cathedral* paintings.
Monet marries Alice, following the death of Ernest Hoschedé the previous year.

1893

Monet continues his work in Rouen.
He buys the plot of land on the far side of the road and obtains permission to excavate a large pond, the first step in the creation of the water garden.

1894

Paul Cézanne comes to Giverny, where he meets Gustave Geffroy, Auguste Rodin and Georges Clemenceau.

1895

Monet travels to Norway. Durand-Ruel exhibits the *Rouen Cathedral* paintings.

1896

Monet paints at Varengeville and Pourville.

1899

Spends time in London.

1900

Returns to London. Durand-Ruel exhibits some ten paintings on the theme of the lily pond, taking the exhibition to New York the following year.

1904

Durand-Ruel exhibits Monet's views of London and the Thames. Monet travels to Spain and London.

1908

Voyage to Venice with Alice.

1909

Exhibition of *Water Lilies* at Durand-Ruel.

1911

Death of Alice Monet.

1912

The Galerie Bernheim-Jeune exhibits Monet's Venice paintings.

1914

Death of Jean Monet, who had married Blanche Hoschedé in 1897.

1915-6

As war rages, Monet builds his third studio, to work on his great 'decorative' paintings.

1918

Georges Clemenceau comes to Giverny, a week after the signature of the Armistice on 11 November.

1922

Signature of Monet's deed of gift to the state of the *Water Lilies* paintings.

1923

Monet has a cataract operation.

1926

Vuillard and Roussel visit Giverny.
On 5 December, Monet dies in the arms of his old friend Clemenceau.

1927

On 17 May, Clemenceau opens the *Water Lilies* exhibition at the Orangerie

Further Reading

First-hand accounts by Monet's guests at Giverny

Georges Clemenceau, *Claude Monet*, 1928; new edition Perrin, 2000.

Marc Elder, *À Giverny chez Claude Monet*, edited and annotated by J.-P. Morel, followed by Claude Monet, *Les Années d'épreuves*, Mille et une nuits, 2010.

Gustave Geffroy, *Monet, sa vie, son œuvre*, introduced and annotated by C. Judrin, followed by *Souvenirs sur Claude Monet, 1889-1909* by Lilla Cabot Perry, Macula, 1980 (see below for English original).

Octave Mirbeau, *Monet et Giverny*, Séguier, 1995

Lilla Cabot Perry, 'Reminiscences of Claude Monet from 1889 to 1909', *Magazine of Art*, 1927

Film:

Sacha Guitry, *Ceux de chez nous*, 1915

Monet and the Impressionists

Marianne Alphant, *Claude Monet, une vie dans le paysage*, Hazan, 1993.

Laurence Bertrand Dorléac, *Contre-déclin. Monet et Spengler dans les jardins de l'histoire*, Gallimard, coll. Art et artistes, 2012.

Pascal Bonafoux, *Claude Monet (1840-1926)*, Perrin, 2007; paperback edition, 2012.

Pierre Georgel, *Water Lilies*, Hazan, 1999.

Marianne Mathieu and Dominique Lobstein, *Monet's 'Impression, Sunrise': The Biography of a Painting*, Yale University Press, 2014.

Sylvie Patin, *Regards sur les Nymphéas*, RMN, 2006.

Sylvie Patin and Anthony Roberts, *Monet: The Ultimate Impressionist*, Thames and Hudson, 1993.

Paul Perrin, 'Autour de Manet et des impressionnistes: Le premier japonisme en peinture', in *Japonismes*, ed. O. Gabet, Flammarion/Musée des Arts décoratifs/Musée d'Orsay/Musée Guimet, 2014, pp. 42-9.

Yves Pouliquen, 'Ah, l'œil de Monet...', in *Monet: L'œil impressionniste*, exhibition catalogue, Hazan/Musée Marmottan-Monet, 2008, pp. 10-20.

Daniel Wildenstein, *Monet's Years at Giverny: Beyond Impressionism*, Harry N. Abrams, 1978.

Daniel Wildenstein, *Claude Monet: Catalogue raisonné*, Taschen GmbH, 1996.

Daniel Wildenstein, *Monet or the Triumph of Impressionism*, Taschen GmbH, 2010.

Major exhibition catalogues

Hommage à Claude Monet, Paris, Galeries nationales du Grand Palais (Hélène Adhémar, Anne Distel, Sylvie Gache [Patin]), RMN, 1980.

Monet: Le cycle des Nymphéas, Paris, musée de l'Orangerie (Pierre Georgel), RMN, 1999.

Claude Monet: 1840-1926, Paris, Galeries nationales du Grand Palais (Guy Cogeval, Sylvie Patin, Sylvie Patry, Anne Roquebert, Richard Thomson), RMN / Musée d'Orsay, 2010.

Claude Monet: Son musée, Paris, musée Marmottan-Monet (Noémie Goldman), Hazan / Musée Marmottan-Monet, 2010.

« Impression, soleil levant ». L'histoire vraie du chef-d'œuvre de Claude Monet, Paris, musée Marmottan Monet (Marianne Mathieu, Dominique Lobstein, Anne-Marie Bergeret-Gourbin, Christian Chatellier, Géraldine Lefebvre et al.), Hazan / Musée Marmottan Monet, 2014.

Monet and Giverny

Geneviève Aitken and Marianne Delafond, *La Collection d'estampes japonaises de Claude Monet*, preface by G. Van der Kemp, La Bibliothèque des Arts/Fondation Claude-Monet, 2007.

Alexandre Duval-Stalla, *Claude Monet, Georges Clemenceau: une histoire, deux caractères*, Gallimard, 2010 ; coll. Folio, 2013.

Franck Ferrand, *Gérald Van der Kemp. Un gentilhomme à Versailles*, Perrin, 2005.

Claire Joyes, *Claude Monet: Life at Giverny*, introduction by G. Van der Kemp, Thames and Hudson, 1985.

Claire Joyes, *Monet's Cookery Notebooks*, Ebury Press, 1996.

Ségolène Le Men (with Cl. Maingon and F. de Maupeou), *La Bibliothèque de Monet*, Citadelles et Mazenod, 2013.

On its cushion in the dining room, the Kutani porcelain cat (Meiji dynasty, 1868-1912) slumbers on.

Calendar of Flowering Times

APRIL: apple blossom (second half of month), aubrietia, azaleas (end of month), campion (second half of month), cherry blossom, clematis (spring-flowering) (end of month), cytisus (broom), daisies (*Bellis perennis*), daffodils and narcissi, forget-me-nots, fritillaries, honesty, hyacinths, pansies and *Viola cornuta*, primroses, society garlic (pink agapanthus ; *Tulbaghia violacea*) (end of month), tamarisk (end of month), tulips, *Erysinum* (second half of month), woad (*Isatis tinctoria*) (second half of month).

MAY: alchemilla, aquilegia, azaleas, campion, clematis (spring-flowering), forget-me-nots, foxgloves, iris (at their peak in the third week), oriental poppies, pansies and *Viola cornuta*, peonies, rhododendrons, society garlic (pink agapanthus ; *Tulbaghia violacea*), sweet rocket (*Hesperis matronalis*), sweet william (*Dianthus barbatus*), tamarisk (beginning of month), thalictrums, tulips (first half of month), *Erysinum*, wisterias, woad (*Isatis tinctoria*) (first half of month).

JUNE: agapanthus, alchemilla, amaranthus, anthemis, aquilegia, bugloss, cleome, clematis, foxgloves, fuchsias, hemerocallis (day lily), impatiens (busy lizzy), lavender, leucanthemum (ox-eye daisy), lilies, nasturtiums, nicotiana (tobacco plant), pansies and viola cornuta, phlox, poppies, roses, society garlic (pink agapanthus ; *Tulbaghia violacea*), sweet williams (*Dianthus barbatus*), thalictrum, water lilies.

JULY: agapanthus, ageratum, alchemilla, amaranthus, anthemis, antirrhinum (snapdragon), clematis (summer-flowering), cleome, coreopsis, corn marigold (*Glebionis segetum*, syn. *Chrysanthemum segetum*), cosmos, dahlias, fuchsias, gladioli, heliotrope, hemerocallis (day lily), hollyhocks, impatiens (busy lizzy), larkspurs, lavender, lilies, nasturtiums, nicotiana (tobacco plant), phlox, pinks and carnations (dianthus, annual and perennial), poppies, roses, rudbeckia (coneflower, black-eyed susan), thalictrum, water lilies.

AUGUST: agapanthus, ageratum, amaranthus, anthemis, antirrhinum (snapdragon), clematis (summer-flowering), cleome, coreopsis, corn marigold (*Glebionis segetum*, syn. *Chrysanthemum segetum*), cosmos, dahlias, fuchsias, gladioli, heliotrope, hollyhocks, impatiens (busy lizzy), larkspur, lavender, nasturtiums, nicotiana (tobacco plant), phlox, pinks and carnations (dianthus, annual and perennial), roses, rudbeckias (coneflower, black-eyed susan), thalictrum, tithonia, verbenas, water lilies, zinnias.

SEPTEMBER: acidanthera (Abyssinian gladiolus, Gladiolus murielae), ageratum, amaranthus, anthemis, antirrhinum (snapdragon), asters, autumn crocus (colchicum autumnale) (second half of month), chrysanthemum, clematis (summer-flowering), cleome, cosmos, dahlias, fuchsias, heliotropes, hibiscus, hollyhocks, impatiens (busy lizzy), lavender, nasturtiums, nicotiana (tobacco plant), phlox, pinks and carnations (dianthus, annual and pernennial), roses, rudbeckias (coneflower, black-eyed susan), sages, sunflowers, tithonia, verbenas, water lilies, zinnias.

OCTOBER: amaranthus, anthemis, antirrhinum (snapdragon), asters, autumn crocus (*Colchicum autumnale*), chrysanthemums, clematis (summer-flowering), cosmos, dahlias, heliotropes, hollyhocks, impatiens (busy lizzy), lavender, nasturtiums, nicotiana (tobacco plant) (some varieties), phlox, pinks (dianthus), roses, rudbeckias (coneflower, black-eyed susan), sages, sunflowers, tithonia, verbenas.

This list is not exhaustive and flowering times are for guidance only. The flowering times of some species may be earlier or later according to weather conditions and changes in climate.

Fondation Claude Monet-Giverny
84, rue Claude-Monet, 27620 Giverny, France

For opening times, access, reservations
and all other practical information, see our website:
www.claude-monet-giverny.fr

Acknowledgments

The author and publisher wish to thank the Académie des beaux-arts, owner of the Fondation Claude Monet, and its permanent secretary M. Arnaud d'Hauterives, Mme Marianne Alphant, Mme Laurence Bertrand Dorléac, M. Laurent Echaubard, M. Guy Cogeval, M. Patrick de Carolis (of the Institut), Mme Laurence des Cars, Mme Madeleine Hanser, Mme Claire Joyes, M. Claude Landais, M. Hubert Le Gall, Mme Claudette Lindsey, M. Fabrice Moireau, Mme Sylvie Patin, M. Paul Perrin, Mme Barbara de Portago, Mr James Priest, M. Gilbert Vahé.

Photographic acknowledgments
All photographs of the house and garden at Giverny: © Éric Sander
p. 5, 17-19 : © Fondation Claude Monet-Giverny
p. 21 : © Collection Philippe Piguet, Paris
p. 24-25, 40-41 : © Fondation Claude Monet-Giverny
p. 26-27, 34-35, 56, 64, 65 bottom, 70, 87 bottom, 91, 92 : © Private Collection, all rights reserved
p. 50 : collection Claire Joyes, all rights reserved
p. 94 : Gilles de Caevel - Manemos.com, © Fondation Claude Monet-Giverny
p. 66 haut : © musée d'Orsay, Dist. RMN-Grand Palais / Patrice Schmidt
p. 57, 76 : © RMN-Grand Palais (musée d'Orsay) / Hervé Lewandowski
p. 86-87 : © RMN-Grand Palais (musée de l'Orangerie) / Hervé Lewandowski
p. 90 : © J.-M. Peers de N; reproduced by permission of the Hoschédé-Monet family
Inside front and back covers and p. 95 : © Fabrice Moireau

ISBN 978-2-35340-213-7 - French
ISBN 978-2-35340-217-5 - English
ISBN 978-2-35340-218-2 - German
ISBN 978-2-35340-219-9 - Japanese
Dépôt légal 2ᵉ trimestre 2015

© Éditions Gourcuff Gradenigo, Paris 2015 - 8, rue des Lilas, 93100 Montreuil, France
© Fondation Claude Monet Giverny - 84, rue Claude-Monet, 27620 Giverny, France

Editor: Xavier Lacaille
Editorial assistant: Raphaëlle Lamy

Translated from the French by Barbara Mellor

www.gourcuff-gradenigo.com
www.claude-monet-giverny.fr

Printed in March 2015
Designed and produced by PAPIER AND CO
for Editions GOURCUFF GRADENIGO
Photogravure and page layout by STIP'ART
Printed by STIPA, Montreuil (France)

5010422